Simple Machines
RAMPS AND WEDGES

David Glover

Heinemann Library
Chicago, Illinois

© 1997, 2006 Heinemann Library
a division of Reed Elsevier Inc.
Chicago, Illinois

Customer Service 888-454-2279
Visit our website at www.heinemannraintree.com

Designed by Victoria Bevan and Q2A Creative
Illustrations: Barry Atkinson (pp. 11, 12, 19) and Tony Kenyon (pp. 5, 9)
Printed in China by WKT Company Ltd.

10 09 08 07 06
10 9 8 7 6 5 4 3 2 1

New edition ISBN: 1-4034-8565-8 (hardback)
                          1-4034-8594-1 (paperback)

The Library of Congress has cataloged the first edition as follows:
Glover, David, 1953 Sept. 4-
     Ramps and Wedges / David Glover.
         p. cm. -- (Simple Machines)
     Includes index.
     Summary: Uses a variety of examples, from scissors and axes to zippers and hairpin turns,
to demonstrate the power of the inclined plane and show how ramps and wedges make work
and play easier.
     ISBN 1-57572-083-3 (library binding)
     1. Simple machines- Juvenile literature. 2. Inclined planes– Juvenile literature.
3. Wedges– Juvenile literature. [1. Inclined planes. 2. Wedges.] I. Title. II. Series: Glover,
David, 1953 Sept. 4– Simple Machines.
TJ147.G58 1997
621.8' 11—dc20

                                                                                    96-17486
                                                                                        CIP
                                                                                        AC

Acknowledgments
The author and publishers are grateful to the following for permission to reproduce photographs:
Trevor Clifford pp. 3, 4, 5, 12, 13, 14, 18, 22, 23; Colorsport pp. 8, 16, 17; Sue Cunningham p. 9;
Mary Evans Picture Library p. 20; J Ringland/TRIP p. 11; Leonard Lee Rue/Bruce Coleman Ltd
p. 15; Robin Smith/TSW p. 21; Jess Stock/TSW p. 7; Zefa pp. 6, 10.

Cover reproduced with permission of Alamy.

The publishers would like to thank Angela Royston for her assistance in the preparation
of this edition.

Every effort has been made to contact copyright holders of any material reproduced in this book.
Any omissions will be rectified in subsequent printings if notice is given to the publisher.

The paper used to print this book comes from sustainable sources.

Contents

Some words are shown in bold, **like this**. You can find
the definitions for these words in the glossary.

What Are Ramps and Wedges?

A ramp is a slope for moving heavy things up and down. It is much easier to push something up a gradual ramp than up a steep one.

When you push something along a ramp, it goes up gradually. You use less effort than when you lift the load straight up into the air.

A wedge is a small ramp that you can move. It is easy to slide a wedge under a door. The wedge **jams** the door open with a large force.

Zigzags

It is hard work to climb a steep hill. You have to lift your body a long way with each step. A **zigzag** path up a hillside takes you steadily to the top. You have to walk farther than if you go straight up, but each step is easier.

Skiers make
zigzag movements
to come down a
steep slope. If they
skied straight down,
they would go too fast
and might crash. The zigzags
help them to come down safely.

FACT FILE Hairpin turns

Roads zigzag up steep hills so that
cars can climb them more easily. The
sharp turns between the zigzags
are called hairpin turns.

Blocks and Chocks

Athletes use wedge-shaped blocks at the start of a race. They are called starting blocks, and they help the runners to push themselves off to a quick start.

This man is using metal wedges to split a block of stone. When he hammers the wedges into the stone, the wedge shape makes the stone split.

Chocks away!

Chocks were once placed under the wheels of airplanes. These wedges stopped the plane from moving until the pilot was ready. When he wanted to take off, he sometimes shouted, "Chocks away!"

Axes and Plows

An ax is a sharp metal wedge that is fixed to a handle. The handle lets you swing the ax head to hit a log with great force. The sharp wedge shape of the ax cuts into the wood and splits it apart.

The first axes

Simple stone axes were made by the first human beings hundreds of thousands of years ago. They tied wedge-shaped pieces of stone to wooden handles.

Farmers use **plows** to turn the soil. A plow has blades that cut into the soil. These blades are metal wedges. They make lines called **furrows**. This tractor is pulling a plow with several blades.

Knives and Scissors

When you cut a carrot with a knife, the blade works as a wedge. The sharp edge of the blade is very thin. It cuts easily into the carrot. The knife blade gets thicker away from the sharp edge. It forces the carrot apart.

Scissors are a pair of blades with sharp, wedge-shaped edges. The blades work together to cut paper or cloth.

Hedge trimmers

A hedge trimmer has lots of wedge-shaped blades. A motor moves the blades back and forth at high speeds.

Pruning shears are powerful scissors with a curved blade. They are used to cut twigs and branches.

Teeth

Feel the shape of your front teeth. They are wedges with sharp edges. You use these teeth to cut and bite your food. You can feel how they work when you take a bite from an apple.

Rats and mice have sharp incisor teeth (see below) for nibbling and gnawing their food. The beavers that live in North America can cut through tree trunks with their powerful wedge-shaped teeth. Beavers use the wood they cut to build their river homes.

Cutting teeth

The eight teeth at the front of your mouth are called incisors. The word incisor means "cutter."

Giant Jumps

This water-skier is jumping off a ramp. The skier comes up to the ramp at high speed. The slope of the ramp lifts her into the air.

This freestyle skier is using a steep snow ramp to jump high into the air. He will be able to make amazing twists and turns before landing.

FACT FILE **Ski jumps**

An expert water-skier can jump half the length of a football field.

Zip It Up!

It is almost impossible to close a zipper without the **slider**. Two wedges inside the slider press the teeth together when you zip it up. A third wedge pushes the teeth apart when you pull the slider down.

FACT FILE Zip invention

The zipper was invented in 1891 by an American named Whitcomb Judson. The first zippers were used to fasten boots.

The teeth on a zipper are shaped so that they fit together, one after the other. A bump on one tooth fits into a dent on the next tooth.

teeth

teeth

slider

wedge

This wedge forces the teeth apart when you undo the zipper.

These two wedges push the teeth together when you pull up the zipper.

Slides and Rides

Some of the most exciting amusement park rides are slopes that you slide down at great speed.

Water rides like this were popular 100 years ago. They are still a lot of fun today. A rope pulls the car to the top of the slope and then lets the car go.

On a roller coaster, your car is pulled to the top of a steep slope by a powerful engine. Then, you rush down the slope on the other side. It is both frightening and exciting at the same time!

Activities

Testing a ramp

1. Make a ramp by balancing one end of a board on some books.
2. Tie a thread or string around a thick book.

3. Pull the book up the ramp.
4. Now, lift the book up in the air using the string. Which is easier—lifting the book or using the ramp?

See page 5 to find out why.

What makes the best doorstop?

1. Open a door. Put a heavy book against the bottom of the door.
2. Can you shut the door?

3. Now, put a wedge under the door. Try to shut the door.
4. Which doorstop works best?

See page 5 for an explanation.

Glossary

chock   wedge-shaped block for putting under wheels to stop them from turning

effort   pushing, pulling, or turning force you must make to move something

furrow   straight cut or groove in the ground that plows make as they turn the soil

jam   to block or wedge in one place

motor   part of a machine that makes it go. Some motors are powered by electricity, others by gasoline.

plow   machine with large blades pulled by a horse or a tractor. A farmer uses a plow to turn the soil in the fields.

pruning shears   cutter that gardeners use to trim bushes and trees

slider   part you move up and down to open and close a zipper

zigzag   line made up of a series of short, quick turns

Index